ON CERTAINTY

Cover art: Cubiculum (bedroom) from the Villa of P. Fannius Synistor at Boscoreale.
The Metropolitan Museum of Art, New York. Rogers Fund, 1903.
www.metmuseum.org/art/collection/search/247017
Cover design by Laura Joakimson
Cover typeface: Athelas

Interior design by Laura Joakimson
Interior typeface: Athelas and Garamond

Library of Congress Cataloging-in-Publication Data

Names: Kelsey, Karla, author.
Title: On certainty / Karla Kelsey.

Description: Oakland, California : Omnidawn Publishing, 2023. | Summary:
"An unnamed woman in an all-too-familiar dystopia narrates *On
Certainty's* story of power and decline, where the Tyrant has gained
ascendency and the Philosopher is dying. Will the narrator take the
Philosopher's place in the struggle against the Tyrant, and in doing so
will she merely perpetuate systemic catastrophe? Here, decimated ecology
is propagated with the Tyrant's android deer, burnt-out towns and
burnt-out lives dependent on virtual reality augmentation. Woven of
speculative fiction, philosophical aphorism, lyric fragment, and
documentary technique, *On Certainty* is like our current moment
simultaneously quotidian and estranged"-- Provided by publisher.

Identifiers: LCCN 2023019296 | ISBN 9781632431202 (trade paperback)
Subjects: LCGFT: Poetry.
Classification: LCC PS3611.E473 O5 2023 | DDC 811/.6--dc23/eng/20230512
LC record available at https://lccn.loc.gov/2023019296

Published by Omnidawn Publishing, Oakland, California
www.omnidawn.com
10 9 8 7 6 5 4 3 2 1
ISBN: 978-1-63243-120-2

ON CERTAINTY

Karla Kelsey

OMNIDAWN PUBLISHING
OAKLAND, CALIFORNIA
2023

For David Bruce Kelsey

1945-2023

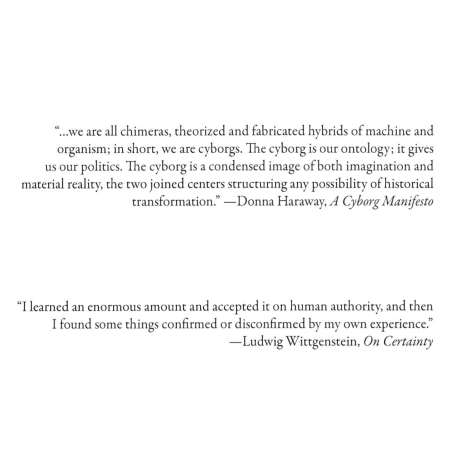

"...we are all chimeras, theorized and fabricated hybrids of machine and organism; in short, we are cyborgs. The cyborg is our ontology; it gives us our politics. The cyborg is a condensed image of both imagination and material reality, the two joined centers structuring any possibility of historical transformation." —Donna Haraway, *A Cyborg Manifesto*

"I learned an enormous amount and accepted it on human authority, and then I found some things confirmed or disconfirmed by my own experience." —Ludwig Wittgenstein, *On Certainty*

...

Chapter ONE

Into the space where the Philosopher had stood I said, a drop of honey
      to lure the bee, what is love
To the Tyrant flashing across the screens of our devices I said, you
      couldn't possibly understand: together we made a series of
      small mirrors, a spit of broken glass

...

The Tyrant had said, great love exists in selecting one thing over all
        others building a villa from what had been a mosque and
        placing, for example, a bed so that through horseshoe-arched
        windows you wake to the sea, a liquor cabinet fitted into the
        mihrab's niche
Or instead of inhaling the bee into a glass container, welcoming the bee
        into the mouth
You should, he says, welcome the bee into your mouth, you should
        welcome the apparatus holding open your mouth while at the
        same time constricting your vocal cords and thus, he says,
        produce silence

     .

What is love, the Philosopher smoothing back his shock-white hair
        had said, but standing naked before the sea's blind gash
        regardless of whether or not the Tyrant and his drones watch

...

Dismissing the screen of my device with a tremor of his paper hand
    the Philosopher had said, the dirt patch where nothing grows
    might yet come into balance
But beauty separating from its context becomes a complicating
    statement
Cruelties of the eye matched by cruelties of the sting
This said while on a wall-sized screen crystalline droplets separate from
    their wave
Love must choose, says a disembodied voice as the droplets separate,
    one thing over all others
In slow motion, again and again, the droplets separate

...

I begin my lecture on the Philosopher's major works saying, before
        the 18th century discovered violet, violets were blue and the
        purple snail was red
I say, Delphic priestesses had been referred to as bees and in Egypt
        bees flew up from Ra's tears
The name of each thing anchors material fragments to time and
        philosophy cannot ignore this
Lecture interrupted: across the screens of our devices the Tyrant
        announces plans for what he's named New City to be built
        frugally and fitted out with virtual reality skins, thus severing
        object from vision
Diazinon, acutely toxic to birds, is sprayed nevertheless over lawns when
        forsythia begins to bloom
We admire the flowers, quietly bury the birds by the shed

     .

The Tyrant taking as had Napoleon Bonaparte the bee *volant en arrière*
        as his insignia

     .

Not until much later will we understand what it means to have seen
        the last of the deer

. . .

I went looking for the sea's blind gash and found the horizon to be
        a brown haze, marine layer refusing dissipation
I found roses dusted with sulfur as bees are woven into wall hangings,
        carpets, upholstery fabrics
"I," then, not pointing to a specific physical or spiritual object but to
        frameworks within which our experience might be described
Waking to find my abdomen slightly furred
The invention of virtual reality skins applied to windows at first a fad for
        changing the view
An instance of *if only*
Constructing a built environment includes the fact that "I," when
        searched for, has yet to be found
Virtual reality skins transform the apartment building before you, its
        satellite dishes and clotheslines exchanged for the sea
Failing bee colonies, we would eventually learn, had been reinvigorated
        by nano drones fitted out with strips of fuzz made from
        horsehair paintbrushes

        .

Even when built frugally with cast concrete panels and steel the practice
        of construction includes future light dawning over rubble and
        thus destruction becomes incorporated into structure
A nano drone taken into the body allows the Tyrant to map his subjects
        from the inside out

...

What is artifice if not a beckoning device, the Philosopher had proposed
        turning his back on the screen and so persuasive with his
        aquiline nose, shock-white hair
Mapping provided by nano drones generates virtual reality skins capable
        of solving the problem of dexterity by hijacking not only the
        reptile brain and prefrontal cortex, but the entire bodily system
Love capable of taking the bee into the mouth
Love a struggle for power and pleasure within a globalized grid
Love regardless of theory you become it and it becomes you
For an entire season the public gardens hold nothing but deadheaded
        roses as across town android deer are sighted in the courtyard
        of the elder home where the Philosopher had just that week
        taken up residence

    .

Time a process that softens rubber, thins glass until generational slashes
        of old flowers reframe what had been objectively established
Seasonal Gardening suggests spraying iris with carbaryl while pinching back
        the plant
I-am-I we know with certainty but what does it mean to believe this

...

I write reality and artifice softly furl into one another, softly mulch
I write to feel my body become lavender and copper and yellow and
    cream
You see, the painting of grapes was so true to nature that birds flew up
    to the wall of the stage
To the wall of the stage I flew up
This is nothing new: the supermarket's white carnations tie-dyed by
        splitting each stem in three sections, each split placed in a vase
        filled with dye and within 24 hours the flower takes up the
        magenta, the turquoise, the yellow
I flew my bird-drone up
Pinks ranging from fuchsia to antique rose in blotches along the throat
How to write philosophy as the freezer fills with bottles containing
        recently collected bees perhaps signifying love had gone

        .

A representation of nature imbued with the power to give arms the
    sensation of wings
Or, if you would prefer: one day we're here the next we're not

...

Chapter TWO

Carbaryl disrupts the insect's nervous system until it fails this is certain

Cicadas in the grass tremoring this is certain

The Philosopher writing what the Philosopher is given to write but
        altered, somehow, by the elder home

This is certain, a softened over-ripe pear

Bringing to the Philosopher instead of the multi-colored carnations a
        small box of foil-wrapped chocolates although the Philosopher
        had always disdained sweets

Collecting specimens from deep in the forest after heavy rain does not
        ensure a natural sample

Teaching my students his earliest texts

        .

There were no, I say to him, real flowers left

...

The Philosopher writing his last text, his death text, his American text
      on certainty we had not been surprised
In history's largest industrial accident 30 tons of poisonous gas produced
      in the manufacture of carbaryl leaks from Union Carbide's
      pesticide plant to its surrounding shanty town in Bhopal, India 1984
The Philosopher continuing in America what had been written abroad
The immediate deaths of 2,259 followed by thousands more

.

Hollyhocks programmed into the wallpaper slightly breathe flaunting,
      we might go so far as to say, our uselessness

.

The West Coast had been overtaken by drought and then fire then flood
The Tyrant inviting us to imagine the architectural wonders of New
      York, Dubai, Beijing, Shanghai, Tokyo projected over simple
      steel and concrete constructions
We know objectively the assertion "I am here" might at any moment
      end
What we had so recently asserted burnt clear by the fires of doubt

...

Let us meditate on the precarity of I-am-I

After all, one simply is or is not

The bees taken from the freezer and dried have of course already
expired

For example, the Philosopher had said, let us revisit our favorite
scenario: likely your father had held the back of the bike steady
as you learned to ride

This now, if it exists, exists as a little home movie of the mind, California
light cast over the drive, a specimen captive behind glass what is
there to say of this

Carbaryl had been discovered and developed in the 1950s by Union
Carbide, a chemical and polymers company whose products
become paints and coatings, packaging, wire and cable,
household products, personal care products, products for the
pharmaceutical, automotive, textile, agriculture, oil, and gas
industries

Pliable branches secured to the ground by nylon ratchet straps

.

Let us appreciate how very far we have come, the Tyrant says, from
the vision of virtual reality administering only the dense flight
or fight experiences of porn and gaming

Separating out the natural from the artificial and then adding natural
specimens to the wasps and winged ants already pinned to agar

...

And then the Philosopher struggling out of his heavy bee-keeping jacket
      says into my recording device: the phrase "I know" falls short
      when confronted by this landscape's limestone masses because
      approached from the east they become the bodies of semi-
      abstracted sculpture, abandoned *kouroi* lounging in a meadow
      just beginning to flower
Union Carbide producing not only common household products but
      also the Bhopal disaster, Hawks Nest Tunnel disaster, Calidria
      chrysotile asbestos mined in California lodged in the lungs
I tap play and he says *the phrase "I know" falls short when confronted by* and I
      tap stop and drag the recording back and I tap play and he says
      the phrase "I know" and I tap stop and drag the recording back
      and I tap play

...

You have a choice, the Tyrant says, to see the world as everyone else
      now sees, augmented by virtual reality skins, or to persist in
      seeing the world alone, as only you see it, dry and brown with
      infrequent patches of blue and green
The question of creation amplified by the fact that we cannot say for
      certain our vulnerability had been intended
The Philosopher's *kouroi* in actuality perhaps mere boulders, perhaps
      mastodon bones, perhaps concrete blocks
I promise, the Tyrant says, you will never choose a return to the
      quotidian

    .

A serpentine mineral sometimes called false jade, Teton jade, Calidria
      chrysotile asbestos fragments into microscopic fibrils that
      released into the atmosphere stick like tiny needles into lungs
When the Philosopher had been young the others wanted to know his
      opinion on thought as a vehicle for being's certainty
A return to the quotidian, the Tyrant suggests with a wry smile, might
      become an alternative form of prison

    .

When collecting bees directly off flowers beware the defense line of the
      sting, throat and abdomen unprotected by bone

...

Chapter THREE

What are we to become when we no longer desire certainty: peonies
        unwilling to be confined to the public garden grow wild along
        the expressway, tactile standards flushed with the meditative
        quality of overlooked things
Staring blankly into the elder home's diorama of Rudolph Zallinger's
        March of Progress I am unable to recall having selected that
        morning the rose-print dress the reflective glass shows me
        to be wearing
The Philosopher unable to explain why the elder home would have
        such a diorama
To what extent does our devotion to paints and coatings, packaging,
        wire and cable, household products, personal care products,
        products of the pharmaceutical, automotive, textile, agricultural,
        oil, and gas industries render us complicit with the Tyrant

        .

I, unable to recall ever having purchased such a rose-print dress
The brash call of the peacock registering in the body as exquisite pain
I, unable to recall developing a fondness for rose-print fabric
I, unable to recall the Philosopher ever previously unable to explain

...

Numerous flawed half-carved *kouroi* lie abandoned in situ within the
     marble quarries of the Greek Cyclades islands
It might well be the case, the Philosopher had said, that we have been
     all along misinterpreting the signs
A pair of sandaled feet, a torso, a face weathering into sand: the words
     "I know that" are always in place when there is no doubt

    .

Egyptian sculpture of the body, based upon mathematical proportions,
     revels in abstract pattern while Greek sculpture of the body,
     based on naturalism, appeals to the eye
Inside architecture's trusses: the double remove of columns that once
     had been trees
When had excess become a sign of decline rather than prosperity
Egyptian calculation so precise one figure, seemingly carved by a single
     artist, might well have been carved by a team of artists working
     in remote locations
My hands are my hands, my breath my breath, and the dusky scent of
     lilies

    .

Upon touch or digestion carbaryl overstimulates insects' nervous
     systems, suppresses the enzyme that would otherwise slow the
     rapid signaling it produces, and thus the nerves continuously
     fire without stopping

...

What can be thought has everything to do with the feather's blue and
        turquoise eye, an iridescence caused by the same process of
        colliding light that produces the brilliance of hummingbirds,
        butterflies, pheasants, birds of paradise
This, embodied by the feather in the jar on the Philosopher's desk
        even as the Philosopher in his chair remains listless
The absurdity of Hominidae, Homo erectus, Neanderthal in *contrapposto*
What can be thought has everything to do with the cry of pain, which
        is not a reflection upon an event but part of hurt itself
And within the sting: proof of a magnificent resistance

    .

The West Coast by drought and then fire and then flood and then
        drought rendered uninhabitable and so designated by the
        Tyrant as a field for nuclear testing

    .

And then silence falling into the Philosopher
Tap play and silence and tap stop

...

New City, the Tyrant's officials have announced, is to be built in the
        country's former heartland
Meanwhile, we no longer say out loud the word *California*
Greek *kouroi* sculpture arises out of Egyptian sculpture shifting from
        two dimensions to three, from surface to volume, from symmetry to
        studied anatomy, stasis to movement
Poppies much larger than your hand are no longer mere physical
        objects but have become a symbol for the absence of balance
The Tyrant owning location, contractors, building materials
Oregon also unspoken
For certainty is, as it were, a matter of tone
Greek artists worked into fragile detail, for example the circa 510 BCE
        Aristodikos kouros has a refined hairstyle, star-patterned pubic
        hair, modeled torso, freestanding arms
To both hate and love who you become in the rose-print dress

    .

Found in over 160 insecticide products carbaryl is commonly sprayed
        on commercial crops such as corn, soybean, cotton, citrus,
        pear and is also applied in suburban yard and garden settings
        because useful in raising and maintaining ornamental and shade
        trees
Washington also lost
The Tyrant merging all virtual reality technology companies with his
        company

    .

The sky injected with an intoxicating shade of rose

...

The Tyrant's investigation into spring cabbage infested by an angular
      cascade of beetles leads to mandated insecticide
New City intends to gloss over the heartland's loss not only of
      agriculture, but also of natural resource extraction and
      manufacturing industry
From the Philosopher's window in the elder home: a garden fitted out
      with a weeping willow and a little wrought iron table and chair
A promise that New City will be disease-free
Or the projected image of a garden fitted out with a weeping willow,
      table and chair, sweating pitcher of iced tea, and the
      remembered certainty of once training heather over a portico
Recent studies show that carbaryl's synthetic chemicals interact with
      human melatonin receptors disrupting circadian rhythms and
      thus raising the risk of diabetes and other metabolic diseases

.

With the slight twist of the head developed by the celebrated *contrapposto*
      of Polykleitos, the direct frontal gaze the Egyptian figure had
      previously exchanged with its viewer had been broken
As if in panic plants grow so fast now, overtaking the greenhouse in
      overabundance

.

What can be thought while sitting next to the Philosopher as he stares
      for what feels like hours into the garden of the elder home

...

But one should not infer, the Philosopher says breaking his silence,
    from the ability to hear even in the midst of cacophony
    hidden compositions, that one is justified in having devoted
    one's life to beauty
A choice of one object over another as humans, animals, forests, fields,
    lakes, seas everywhere are dying
And certainly it is an error, the Philosopher says, and an arrogance to
    infer that one is justified in devoting one's life to philosophizing
    beauty even as one becomes increasingly skeptical about the
    possibility of choice
Grazing in the garden: the android deer
Upon returning home the rose-print dress quickly taken off, shoved into
    the back of the armoire

...

Chapter FOUR

For the Philosopher I describe the new advertisement projected across
      the university administration building featuring the Tyrant in
      navy suit, white shirt, orange tie, arms outstretched sowing roses
      and chrysanthemums over the fields of the former heartland
We once found our location by Polaris, its height above the horizon
      measured by sextant or fist the means by which we understood
      our latitude
The roses and chrysanthemums first growing and then evolving into
      simple buildings of steel and concrete blocks
We once found location in the relationship between fortune and rule,
      the ancient Greeks and Romans understanding the area around
      each settlement to be alive
The Tyrant then conducting virtual reality skins modeled after the
      Freedom Tower, Burj Khalifa, China Zun, Oriental Pearl, Mode
      Gakuen Cocoon Tower to wrap his simple steel and concrete
      constructions
Building a city, as ancient cultures knew, disturbs equilibrium, wounds
      the place and the life that must sustain it in visible and invisible
      ways
New City advertisements play on a loop over the façades of the old city

     .

Location after the death of the Philosopher nearly impossible to imagine
There is wounding and there is re-wounding
The approaching death of the Philosopher, brought into focus by the
      elder home, nearly impossible to imagine

...

Chairs on only three sides of each dining hall table: wheelchair parking,
       the Philosopher had said taking me by surprise the afternoon
       he wheeled, rather than walked, up to the table in the elder
       home
To what extent is it possible for a virtual sea to provide access to an
       actual sea, which might or might not be already lost
Unsatisfied by the then-young Philosopher's refusal to answer his
       question about thought as grounds for being's certainty, an
       esteemed elder philosopher, now long deceased, had left with
       a flurry of his scarf, banging the lecture hall door
Or so the story goes
The meaning of a word is a glossary dependent on its array of relations
       which are facts but might or might not be things
Of course the "I" cannot be rendered entirely unimportant regardless
       of its fictive properties

.

A field recording of wind conveys the seabed after water had been
       diverted, camels wandering past skeletons of ships
I again catching my reflection in a rose-print dress
Under night sky we come into relation with landscape's dream of
       lavender and copper and yellow and cream

...

That the statement "There is a fire in this room and I don't believe
  that there is" doesn't contain a formal contradiction suddenly
  becomes self-evident when considering the statement "There
  is a person I love in this room and I don't believe in love"
The Tyrant, California, New City, virtual reality skins: a list of topics
  rarely spoken of in the elder home
Too preoccupied, the Philosopher said, with the rapid transformation
  of body and mind
The window may well give on to a parking lot, the dress may well be
  made of plain linen
That the esteemed elder philosopher had died one week later was said
  to prove the possibility of death by disappointment the
  younger Philosopher, now old, told me tucking his napkin
  into his collar
An advertisement suggests collecting asteroids in the rings of Saturn
The I increasingly not-I

...

Or consider, the Philosopher said jabbing with his spoon the surface
        of his jello, a lilac leaf cross-sectioned and viewed under
        a microscope
Revealed: green crescents and spheres, palisade cells, emerald vistas
And yet just a moment ago we had been consumed by the panicles'
        scent, cloying and too sweet
Not only that: the brain continually turns the retina's upside-down
        image right-side up
Intuited: the betrayal the esteemed elder philosopher had felt over the
        then-young Philosopher's refusal to answer the question was
        the betrayal of first love
The single figure seated upside-down in a lilac-sequined dress contains
        frost's mutation and movement
We can imagine but cannot know the elder philosopher's surprise at
        the sensation of betrayal, his further shock in tracing this
        sensation back to what must be, he must have surmised, the
        blush of first love, an experience he had heretofore been
        certain he had permanently avoided
Which might propose, the Philosopher had said, virtual reality as
        merely an instantiation of what already transpires in the
        human mind

...

In the hallway: a rainbow produced by projecting light through fine
       mist or the sensation of a rainbow produced by projecting
       light through fine mist
One of the Tyrant's Representatives in navy suit, white shirt, orange
       tie visiting the elder home saying even if deer are never to be
       seen again we have a reservoir of deer images: cave paintings,
       etchings, taxidermy, documentary videos, kitschy statuettes,
       art objects
The younger Philosopher became the older Philosopher looking to a
       younger philosopher such as myself to address his questions
       of architecture and time
The Representative saying to the elders gathered in the activity room:
       we are now in the age not of materiality which is as you intimately
       know always disintegrating, but of information
       which increases in abundance more rapidly than its body
       deteriorates
The Representative then handing out postcards of Kōhei Nawa's 2011
       PixCell-Deer #24, a taxidermy deer covered with spheres of
       artificial crystal glass
Handing out postcards of a body proportioned not by nature but as if
       by an imagined hand

      .

Wheeling from the activity room with a flurry of his scarf the
       Philosopher had the sensation that he had once before
       performed this exact same gesture

...

Building a house, the Philosopher had said, is not unlike dressing: one
       makes artificial skins and wraps them around a body
The taxidermy deer and its crystal spheres meant to conjure an organic
       pixel sensation
Earth as body as pollen begins to fall
Oystershell scales on both willows and lilac should be pruned out,
       only then might the question arise: what must happen in the
       larger world such that the Tyrant will quit the idea that he
       makes it rain
What might be taken as fact worthy of conversion into sense

     .

Instead of building a house I thought of the spores patterning the
       undersides of ferns
I thought plant gall and tumor
I thought absence of both questions and answers
I thought of the Philosopher in his wheelchair making the gesture
       of the long-dead elder philosopher by leaving with a flurry
       of his scarf
An invisible dynamic becomes visible, nature slamming the door with
       exactly the same sound

...

Chapter FIVE

I should perhaps state plainly that despite my distaste for chaos I'm in
      no hurry to expunge doubt

This felt in the sacrum, crux of the vertebral column, part-pelvis and
      part-spine

Carved *contrapposto* preparing for her bath and discarding her robes
      with one hand while shielding her womanhood with the
      other, Praxiteles' *Aphrodite of Knidos* erected in 360 BCE was
      perhaps the first Greek female nude sculpture

Uncertainty a necessary component for establishing an experience of
      coming into being and passing away

Centerpiece to a circular temple overlooking the sea and open on all
      sides to provide a 360-degree view of the nude

I was uncertain, for example, of edges, folds, translations, disintegrations
      into the place where what I thought of as "myself" ceases and
      "the world" begins

Carved of fine-grained semi-translucent pure white and entirely flawless
      Parian marble

Despite the desire to be otherwise

...

Original lost to time, we know *Aphrodite of Knidos* only by description and
    imitation
Propagation by crown division a slow mechanism reflecting the
    propensity to be multiplied by photograph, postcard, print-
    maker, copyist, virtual reality
The statue is rumored to be modeled upon Phryne, Praxiteles' lover and
    a famous *hetaera,* courtesan, mistress who had first caught the
    artist's eye as she undressed at a festival, taking her hair down as
    she walked into the sea

    .

The endless replication of the celebrity Pop art face without a body in
    Andy Warhol's portraits of Marilyn Monroe, Jackie Kennedy,
    Elizabeth Taylor perhaps constitutes the ideal American nude

    .

And yet even in absence *Aphrodite of Knidos* exerts such influence one
    might believe each and every subsequent Western female nude
    to be a reinterpretation

    .

Awakening with a coronet of wild flowers unpetaling in one's hair
    while knowing for certain one hadn't been in any garden

...

I woke to find myself wearing an acanthus-print dress in a meeting
        room done up with acanthus-print wallpaper, carpet, curtains
Unable to ask what happened to California
Upon the closing of pagan temples in 392 CE *Aphrodite of Knidos* likely
        had been taken to Constantinople and displayed in a palace
        museum until destroyed by fire in 476 CE
To be an absence known by imitations scattered across the
        Mediterranean, deducing one's own image from replicas
        created in various shapes and sizes formed of marble, clay,
        limestone, bronze, each bearing slightly different proportions
And imagining this absence, feeling the shape of her body, I thought
        what is a gesture of love
I thought the *Medici Venus, Capitoline Venus, Melian Aphrodite, Crouching
        Aphrodite, Sandal-binding Aphrodite, Aphrodite Anadyomene,
        Capuan Aphrodite, Aphrodite of Arles, Aphrodite Kallipygos*
        otherwise known as *Venus of Beautiful Buttocks*
Standing before *PixCell-Deer #24* in a museum I thought about the
        android deer in the elder home parking lot, thought about
        the Philosopher sitting in the garden, blanket tucked around
        his legs, clematis trained over the chain-link fence

...

During this season's rumor of aphids the Tyrant requires malathion
        to be sprayed along the underside of foliage
The soft white interior of my arms: acanthus-printed
Venus Colonna, housed in the Vatican and considered the most authentic
        copy, critiqued for being too fleshy, stodgy, flabby to have been
        an exact imitation
And thus one remains silent, unable to catch the Representative by his
        sleeve and so night after night returning home before the
        firework display's 300 shells spitting out pyrotechnic stars in
        celebration of the month the Tyrant had been born
To sleep requires both eyeshade and earplugs against red and amber,
        titanium and brocade-gold
Waking to my pubic hair star-patterned, my torso tattooed with red
        and violet blooms

...

The activity room wall of the elder home projected with the firework
        display as witnessed from a drone's-eye view

At this point in the season evergreens can still be planted, rhododendron
        and azalea infected with lace bugs should be sprayed with
        malathion or diazinon *Seasonal Gardening* suggests

Chickens bred without cerebral cortexes an attempt to separate meat
        from information

To burst with the fire-flower from within, to become an amber cascade
        of sparks: a longing to lend the surface negligence is not so very
        different from a longing to lend the surface intelligence

An article on colony collapse recalls the sensation of drawing the bee
        into the glass jar so similar to drawing the bee into one's own
        mouth

How to resist the Tyrant's closets of unworn shirts and in every district
        seizing for his own an apartment complete with a wife, son,
        daughter, staff ready-to-hand, at each periphery a woman
        appointed to be his mistress

His possessions monogramed with bees, he makes speeches about the
        decadence of libraries, museums, universities

.

The Philosopher saying as the nurse pulls the privacy curtain: we have
        yet to become pure information

Shredded into nests or torched with lighter fluid and match

Chapter SIX

...

A silver gelatin print of the Pacific depicts nothing but water, light,
       and air, yet its metallic weight references the 10 million tons
       of plastics dumped into the ocean each year
References the coastline flooded, fields droughted out
We speak about experience as it manifests through the body and try
       but cannot succeed in translating ourselves into abstract
       systems
The spine, for example, akin to a cairn of stones, relies on the sacrum
       to establish balance
Loose sand and agricultural toxins cyclone over the basin
By "lost" we mean "completely uninhabitable"
First one university closes and then another and another
Yet substance and process transmute into vision, framing catastrophic
       shift with familiarity
Projected on the activity room wall: fireworks illuminating the Bay of
       Naples, Vesuvius quiet in the background as the Philosopher
       confesses he now rarely sleeps
The sea has birthed a desert, the desert has birthed a valley, a valley
       of shifting sands

          ·

We are, the Philosopher says, excess energy released as sacral silk
So little organic flora remains, so little organic fauna
What is the self but another body soon lost

...

Without a doubt one would like to say one knows for certain that the
      body one inhabits is one's own, has been one's own since
      birth
Such foundations of thought prevent sowing your favorite sweet corn
      all the while expecting something other than corn might
      follow
Crossette, horsetail, dahlia, diadem, willow, roman candle

    .

Defining the concept "sense of embodiment" begins simply: one's self
      is located inside a body
I look into the mirror with surprise: a flattening of the facial plate, fur
      around the temples, and yet: I-am-I
This in contrast with the detached formalism of a graph depicting the
      half-life of chemicals telling me very little of what I long to
      know

    .

The struggle for meaning a struggle between pleasure and power
After fireworks: residue of heavy metals, ozone, sulfur dioxide, and
      other toxins floating down
To be a figure in the tide garnering debris from sea caves, beaches,
      estuaries
To call on one's own "sense of embodiment" as the primary vehicle of
      certainty, discarding my robes with one hand while shielding
      my sex with the other

    .

The self beyond death: a class of life without a name

...

Nerves work by signaling to each other via chemical messengers

The body where I perceive myself, where I find my self to be located
is self-defined: the body in which "I perceive myself to be" is
the body in which "I am"

But if truth were told, any understanding we possess is most like latticed
fungi buried in soil, a network by which trees send and receive
nutrients

Identity determined by its totality of relations, that is to say, by
everything that it is not

The event and the narrative of the event

.

Our account of the 79 CE eruption of Mount Vesuvius was written by
Pliny the Younger: lodging at the house of his uncle Pliny the
Elder in Misenum across the Bay of Naples he witnesses the
eruption that obliterates Pompeii

Fungi transmit warning signals at approaching environmental shift

In addition: the account articulated by impressions left by bodies
encased in volcanic ash

Trees transfer their nutrients to other plants when death is near

...

For nearly a full minute after display: thin strokes mark the sky with
       heather and the expressway lined with virtual reality's verdant
       fields seems so true to nature we expect the deer's return
For nearly a full minute after display: Earth imaged as a pear-wood ball
       suspended in night-blue bunting and doves fly up to the wall of
       the stage to eat at a vine painted across the proscenium
Yet clearly this cannot compensate for the grapevines slowly dying
Pliny the Younger writes of his uncle having been out in the sun, having
       taken a cold bath, lunched, and settling down to work on the
       Naturalis but then interrupted by his sister drawing his attention
       to a cloud of smoke across the bay
Interacting with a landscape sprayed with malathion the nerve system
       fires without stopping until the insect, unable to move or
       breathe, dies
A plume 20 miles high thrusting upwards and then splitting off into
       branches like an umbrella pine

     .

Furthermore, underlying our sense of embodiment is the certainty that
       this body, "my" body, obeys the self's, "my" self's, intentions
The body operating much like a remote-controlled unit, but from within

...

What is love but nerve signals firing without stopping
Each day after meeting with students a noon visit to the elder home
Such a conceptually simple "sense of embodiment" complicates when
        we define the body as a container, which in the context of
        virtual reality might be any object
As of late, when I'm not turned by the nurses away I sit bedside
        watching the Philosopher slip in and out of twilight
Just as it acts on insects malathion works on people, pets, and other
        animals and while considered to have low toxicity, children with
        higher levels of the pesticide in their system are at greater risk
        for ADHD
Before dying the Philosopher hypothesized: if the ground is well-
        prepared for unsettling, notions such as "the original" or "the
        dream of the real" will be replaced by virtual reality skins,
        unabashed and reveling in artifice
Pliny the Elder calls for a boat to be prepared so that he might as a man
        of science investigate
When researchers fed malathion to rats for two years they found no
        evidence of increased cancer
Receiving a message from a house at the base of Vesuvius he learns the
        mountain has begun to convulse and the only way out is by sea
      .

The activity room wall overlayered with a view of the coast of Italy from
        Pompeii to Naples, past and present, flashing red and amber,
        titanium and brocade-gold

...

Chapter SEVEN

In Jeff Koons' virtual reality experience *Phryne* you encounter a shiny
    metallic Jeff Koons ballerina in a lavish garden and immediately
    you undergo the strong feeling that she is aware of you
Revising his mission from science to rescue, Pliny the Elder gathers a
    fleet of warships, traverses the bay to those trapped between fire
    and water
To collect clusters of clover-like blooms creates a first-order experience
    as does drinking petals seeped as a tea and rumored to detoxify
    the liver, reverse aging, improve sight
If you come close enough to touch the ballerina you somehow enter her
    world, pierce the membrane of her skin, and her body becomes
    your body
In an attempt to discover whether or not the eruptions of Vesuvius had
    been witnessed from the North African coast one must take an
    overnight ferry from Naples to Palermo and then on to North
    Africa: Tunis, then Bizerte

.

Upon entering the body of another, one's "sense of embodiment"
    transplants, regardless of the fact that the other is virtual
Or the train to Salerno and the 24-hour ferry to Tunis and then on
    to Bizerte
Although we thought we knew the difference between ornament in
    architecture on the one hand and gesture in physical movement
    on the other, the fact of the dove bursting from sky to angle
    down into the theater of representation thrills not for its deceit
    but for wings beating so close to the ear

.

This I say to the Philosopher or read to the Philosopher or say in my
      head to the Philosopher or read silently in my head to the
      Philosopher

...

An account of ash falling hot and thick as the ships drew near followed
        by 18 hours of pumice and blanched stones, charred and
        cracked by flame
Then suddenly shallow water and the shore blocked by debris
Then avalanches of *saxa liquefacta,* hot molten lava streaming from the
        crater at enormous speed
The ferry ride an attempt to see with the clarity of *PixCell-Deer #24's*
        spheres of crystal glass
Pliny the Younger as if inhabiting his uncle's body describes broad
        sheets of fire and flame, pumice stone raining down and in
        the middle of the day a darkness blacker and more dense than
        any woolen sheet
Or the ferry ride an attempt to discover whether or not traces of the
        Tunisian revolution are still evident
We might, my students suggest, trace these traces

    .

Inside the virtual body of Jeff Koons' ballerina is another garden where
        you find another ballerina

...

Pierce the body of this ballerina and you will find yourself inside another
      garden

An ecstatic blindness to the context of the painted pile of grapes

The Philosopher then three decades younger although seeming to me
      with his shock-white hair already old and I, a student so young,
      so quiet, together had almost daily wandered the university
      garden lined with palms and bougainvillea, California coastal
      light

An ecstatic blindness to the system of propositions that underlie belief,
      but what remains after loss

Dramatizing Pliny the Younger's account we have the famous figures of
      Pompeii created by the excavators of 1860 who poured plaster
      into the soft ash depressions formed by bodies in their moment
      of death

We also have the preserved frescoes of the Roman villas dotting the
      eastern slopes of Vesuvius as it eddies down to the sea

For example the Villa of P. Fannius Synistor, foundation remains located
      in suburban Boscoreale, walls painted with cities, ports, terraced
      houses, projecting balconies, gods, goddesses, gardens, buried
      upon Vesuvius' eruption, 79 CE

The architect of the Villa, like the architect of the metallic ballerina, like
      both the Philosopher and the Tyrant: unabashed

     ·

And later: virtual reality skins transform the view of blighted crops and
      burnt-out cities into vineyards, villages, shining mirrored
      skyscrapers

...

If we graph projected climate change the phrase "final planting" takes
      on new resonance

The Philosopher then three decades younger in the university garden
      looking at me squarely in the eyes and so close I could smell the
      sweet tobacco smoke embedded in his corduroy coat had said,
      desire articulates concepts heretofore unrecognized

The sex of shell flowers and tuberoses then arranged themselves as
      perpetual fire

And what if the ballerina's body seems to be my body, and the garden's
      body my body, and the body inside that garden my body, and
      your intention is to move from body to body and in so doing
      pierce and pierce and pierce

A flaw in logic: assuming that because past civilizations have withstood
      natural and social catastrophe we too will withstand natural and
      social catastrophe

In passing through such truths I come into being just as the ferry docks
      among wide white walls and minarets

...

Knowledge of what one is doing, like knowledge of one's opinion, is
       non-observational but might be felt, nevertheless, as flushed
       skin, elevated pulse, the body in 3-D panorama
However: one cannot be certain whether the wide white walls and
       minarets are virtual or real, informational or material

    .

To find one's way through a phrase, which is to find one's way through
       a body, location, character, one must begin relinquishing the
       sensation of ownership
Standing with the Philosopher then three decades younger, the same age
       as I am now, looking from California bluffs now ravaged to the
       once turquoise and violet sea
In response to collapse: virtual planting
In response to deterioration: memory

...

The Philosopher's advice dictated from his elder home bed: form a
      sense of location, a sense of self as a pear-wood ball floating
      free in space
A model of Earth complete with oceans of lapis inlay
In memory, the university garden, the opening sex of flowers, a dryness
      to the mouth
The nurse drawing closed the privacy curtain
If virtual reality technology can give rise to the sensation of California's
      mariposa lilies, Mexican shell flowers, coppertips, will I try to
      bring the Philosopher back to me
We had been programed to want gardens planted for gracefulness as
      well as color and intended to create a simple picture nearly
      impossible to doubt
I touch my sacrum, bend slightly my back: I do not know these will be
      the last words we will have from the Philosopher
And within these gardens other forbidden gardens of fleshy flowers,
      thorns, the vines themselves conscious, sensuous, tendriling the
      body with pleasure

     .

Bedroom walls painted with cities, porticoes, balustrades, pergolas,
      columns, friezes, theater masks, mythological and allegorical
      figures
A woman among roses in a rose-print dress
What force are you willing to use to access the garden
Real walls dematerializing under the illusion that space has been
      extended into jewel-toned cities

...

An image is something visible by which we see something less
      immediately self-evident: the movement of planets relatively
      easy to predict, the movement of animals nearly impossible
Sitting bedside in the elder home not so much thinking as the
      Philosopher hovers in a twilight state about the university
      garden, which I hadn't thought of in years, but reliving it,
      movie-like, the sun hot the sea bright his hand on my arm and
      then pressing his lips to my lips pressing me into the garden's
      cool stone wall
A division of global consciousness between those who remember a time
      prior to the iconic Blue Marble shot rendering our planet whole
      and illuminated and floating alone and those who have always
      recognized this image to be an uncanny representation of home
Or the power of the image and the idea of the image: the 2010 self-
      immolation of Mohamed Bouazizi inspiring the Tunisian
      revolution, which inspired the Arab Spring
Let us pause here, my students said, we need to study this

...

Chapter EIGHT

The Tyrant appearing on screen in a digital remake of Tinto Brass's 1979
     Caligula: gold foil crown, crotch-high tunic, white horse, blackbird
     imprisoned in mesh
Malathion is highly toxic to the fruit fly, bollworm, mosquito, bee, and
     the gills of walleye, trout, bluefish deteriorate after 24 hours of
     exposure
The sun too hot he tasted of stale coffee, tobacco, sour milk
Pesticides reach water-bearing aquifers below ground from application
     onto crops, seepage of contaminated surface water, accidental
     spills, improper disposal, injection of waste into wells
The image field proliferates with flawless blossoms when you Google
     a flower's name
The sensation that extinct flora and fauna have been brought back to life

          .

Our habits of belief demonstrated by our relationship to visual imagery:
     in what ways does the body register a distinction between virtual
     and non-virtual reality
To deny oneself the garden

...

Right before your eyes: not the ravaged volcano of today but Vesuvius
        as it had been over 2,000 years ago, green forests below the
        summit and farther down, wild animals roaming oak and beech
The brutality of love little else than stripping away illusory robes of I-
        am-I
To zoom in on a pair of deer grazing the first-century vetch
We might easily trace an effect back to its cause but have much more
        difficulty projecting the possible effects of any given gesture
The sun, the sea too bright with it
The Tyrant assuming the body of Caligula, Caligula of pleasure barges
        and talking to the moon, of ordering to be built an altar to
        himself, a brothel in the imperial palace, treason trials,
        expansionist campaigns
The lower slope's fertile volcanic soil planted with olives and grapes

...

The cities of Pompeii and Herculaneum at Vesuvius' base were built
according to the position of the sun: wide streets ran east to
west following its path, narrow north-south streets ran in the
direction of Earth's axis

A 3-D model now provides us with a sense of the structure of the Villa
of P. Fannius Synistor: three stories including baths and
agricultural quarters arranged in a square around the peristyle

Turned away by the elder home from the Philosopher's room, *at this
point family only,* and so recalling the Philosopher three decades
ago in the university garden having pressed me against the cool
stone wall saying the world and the life are one, and kissing me
and hard against me, and saying you are a reflective surface
expansive and permeable

.

Some things are confirmed: continents, weather patterns, seas

And some things are disconfirmed: gods, for example, hovering with the
drones and satellites

...

The manufactured sensation of a meadow blossoming in contrast to a
       galaxy of goldflame spirea, beauty bush, butterfly weed, and all
       the insects these varieties attract
Volcano, violence, violetry: what love and terror might attract
What is love
While there is no hard evidence, Caligula is said to have had incestuous
       relationships with all three of his sisters
The soon-to-be ousted Tunisian President visiting Bouazizi in hospital
       just prior to his death: a tribute or an attempt to harness an
       image's power
The spatial distinction marked and constituted by a cell membrane is
       chemical and energetic, permeable and forever-vibrating
Did the soon-to-be ousted Tunisian President ask Bouazizi if his body in
       the act of self-immolation willingly obeyed the revolution
       visioned by his mind
The sensation of bees brought back by miniature drones performing the
       bee function for flowers

...

Caligula on the way to the baths was jumped by members of the
        Praetorian Guard: 30 blows and a rumor that the assassins ate
        his flesh
Pictorial space, agricultural space, virtual space
Again turned away and spotting the android deer as I made my way
        down the drive
Volcano, violence, violetry: the "where" of coming into being, even if
        never thought, becomes substratum anchoring meadow garden,
        high garden, lavender garden, flowers pulling through the trash
        and the dirt

    .

Leafing through a book and pausing on a photograph of the
        Philosopher three decades younger at his chalkboard, at his
        proofs, his shock-white hair and surrounded by his circle of
        students, I half out of the shot
The Philosopher soon after resigning his post at one university and
        taking up a post in another university on a different continent
Pictorial reality, agricultural reality, virtual reality

...

Factors such as season, time of day, and whether a person strolled,
    entertained, or slept in any given interior informed the
    decoration of each space composing the Villa's structure
This, in contrast with the cocoon-like dwelling I assign in an attempt
    to keep the bird in focus while seeing the landscape all at once
The Philosopher existing for decades only in the form of letters,
    manuscripts, essays, monographs
Zooming in and out via Google Earth
The Philosopher long having been part-virtual was no less an intimate
    component of my life
Cultivating an energy, as in a still life where all objects occupy the same
    existential plane
Beginning my career writing my texts on his texts

    .

To become, in the end, what exists in others' memories
Yet daily the world-picture although remaining unmentioned influences
    the decision to spray weekly with Cygon 2E, harmful or fatal if
    swallowed by humans, domestic animals, wildlife, aquatic
    vertebrates, insects

    .

Entering Jeff Koons' *Phryne* to pierce the ballerina's bright metallic body
    and assume the contours of her limbs do we trouble ourselves
    with the question of where "she" goes when we become her
The skeletal structure of space known by touch and created by the
    movement of hands

...

Cuttings of pinks, inserted in sandy soil, burn

Unbidden, the movie-mind plays the clip of the Philosopher reappearing
nearly a decade ago in the airport's arrivals terminal, brown
corduroy jacket, shock-white hair, tobacco-sweet as if he had
never left

By then we had learned to live under the conditions of the Tyrant: that
the touch of his hands had proven to be virtual rather than
material, a scant consolation

The Philosopher as if he had never left declaring the idea of dwelling
as doll house and architectural model to be a violence done
unto caves and uncharted wilderness

Perpetual carnations given their final potting presuppose something we
haven't yet known

The idea of an other located between memory and touch

Turned away again from the elder home, to the Tyrant on the screen I
make the curtsy of the metallic ballerina and then I give him the
bird, the chin-flick, the fig, the fuck-off

The turn-of-the-century excavators of villas built among Vesuvius' olive
groves and orchards were more interested in collecting
household objects, statues, and frescoes to sell than
documenting village and villa structures

Reduced to impotent gestures how do we begin to rebuild the moving
body

There is no corner of Earth, the Tyrant boasts, no fold, no cave, no
basement, no bunker unobserved by satellite

The Villa even while buried in ash insisted upon yellow ochre, cinnabar
red

...

Allowed entrance to what had been the Philosopher's room at the elder
       home only to find the bed stripped, personal effects neatly
       bundled into plastic bags bearing the elder home's butterfly logo
The house dismantled
Humanity pressed into artifact

     .

After excavation sites were reburied under dirt, the land returned to
       agriculture
The space between expected death and death as quiet as a blizzard

...

Chapter NINE

To mistake the love of artifacts for the love of a lost civilization

The frescoes of the Villa of P. Fannius Synistor sold to muscums in
    New York, Naples, Brussels, Amsterdam

Minimalism turned maximal: Cygon 2E used to control lace bugs,
    leafminers, mites, tea scales, white flies, aphids, thrips is
    approved for use on azaleas, birch, boxwood, camellias,
    hemlock, junipers, roses, beans, broccoli, leaf lettuce, spinach,
    kale, Swiss chard, melon, peas, potatoes, tomatoes

A body tossed by breakers forms a more intimate relationship with the
    sea than a body on the sand gazing out

.

The early 20th-century excavators who re-buried the Villa's erotic
    frescoes and artifacts were uncertain of the market for Priapus
    with his outsized penis, Pan copulating with goats, a continuous
    row of phalluses decorating the tops of gates and walls

Body pressed into salt

...

The gods and goddesses have fled, but a 3-D model now provides us
    with a sense of the Villa's structure: three stories including
    baths, agricultural quarters, and an underground passage with a
    stable in which a horse during the volcanic eruption had been
    trapped
I tap play and he says *the phrase "I know" falls short* and I tap stop and drag
    the recording back

    .

To lie in bed late morning listening to birds singing I-not-I, there-not-
    there
To lie in bed late morning listening to nature tapes
To find oneself in the mind's eye standing before the Villa's fresco
    depicting a bull's head nailed to lavish red cladding, an animal
    appearing amazingly alive

    .

Pearls wrapped around his horns, heavy swags tied to his ears, a hole in
    his forehead, slightly opened eyes: these attributes suggest he
    had just been decapitated for sacrifice

    .

Venus depicted stepping out of the sea, lower body reminiscent of
    Aphrodite of Knidos with the upper body of the *Medici* and
    Capitoline Venuses

    .

To lie in bed first in the body of a woman and then in the body of a man
    and then in the body of a lion, bear cub, deer
The body as building wrapped in virtual reality skins

    .

I tap play and I tap stop

...

From within the bright white rectangle of grief "virtual" and "actual"
     become a matter of strategy
I entered the virtual reality model and knelt
The future predicted in a painted detail of the Villa's wall: a bowl filled
     with peaches, quinces, green almonds, figs all visible thanks to
     transparent blown glass, a technology not yet known to Italy
I held my hands up as if violet, as if olive, as if coral
Pliny the Elder's body, smoke-choked, found on the shore fully clothed
     and looking more like sleep than death
I watched the Philosopher leaving the lecture hall with a flurry of his
     scarf
Frescoes between columns depict illusionistic trees, birds, and in the
     western corner a household shrine holding statuettes and floral
     offerings

     .

I watched a tear in the veil of time
I watched a god rambling down to disappear in the sea
I watched a volcano shudder forth tephra and gasses, molten rock,
     pulverized pumice, and out of the hot ash the Tyrant rises

...

To awaken, my skin rose-patterned and not remembering having
        consented to such augmentation

I point to the world or I point to a framework for understanding the
        world

The term *nota* is used for what's in the mouth of the speaker, *signum* for
        what's in the ear of the listener

The two of necessity differ

A miniature glass deer wrapped in tissue paper a gift from the Tyrant
        upon the death of the Philosopher

My students knock and I don't answer and they knock and I don't
        answer and they stop

To prevent black spots and rust spray Maneb or Zineb at cluster, pink
        bud, petal fall, fruitlet stage

Possible attitudes toward the conviction that one's framework and the
        world exactly match: to awaken to disjunction, to remain asleep
        to disjunction, to act a sudden storm making havoc of, among
        other things, the careful border of carnations

.

O Blue Marble dashed against cosmic energy fields, excavation ditch
        revealing two lovers and their horse

...

About things and events themselves there may be little or nothing to say
Yes, the starting point may seem small, obvious, but consider the
          importance of whether or not you dig your plot in actual or
          simulated dirt
The girl wearing the virtual reality headset, scissors in her hands
          snapping at air might constitute both excess and lack at the self-
          same time
You are not, the Philosopher would have said to me upon detecting my
          sorrow, unique
And silence might constitute an excess or lack of significance
And an abundance might constitute advancement or degeneration
It is the lot of the human to lose everything, I imagine him saying, and
          so don't force me, he says shaking back his shock-white hair, to
          speak in platitudes we are both, he says, too tired, too old, too
          something for that
Along the wall a bank of headsets donned by a group all at once there is
          a metaphor in this
Reflecting the scaffolding of our thoughts, roses and dahlias disbudded
          with small snips, the strain of moving away from landscapes
          into arenas of virtual abstraction
What they see we cannot know: some members of the group wince in
          pain, some sink to the ground, a boy bends vomiting, a woman
          in a pantsuit laughs

          .

I was most comforted when situated in the body of a deer wandering the
          elder home garden, grazing on the fallen fruit at the base of Vesuvius

...

Virtual reality's control of the landscape amounts to the sensation of
        controlling time
Out the window the shadows shift when they are told to shift
Out the window the nude walks by when she is told to walk by
Now donning the skin of a man, a boy, a grandmother, a panther,
        a rabbit
And the hour first on slow and then sped up
If you haven't figured yourself into an image yet, if you haven't yet
        stripped the rose of its thorns as it transfers from the arms of
        Venus to the arms of the Madonna of the Arbor, the image field
        will overtake you, making you its own

        .

What we understand by identifying marks, a mole near the eye, a scar
        on the hip, are the instances in which an object hopes to be
        recognized as what it is, distinguished from all other objects
The rumor that some of us never had been human was first circulated
        with amusement, then with terror, then with acceptance

        .

I looked in the mirror and saw my body to be the metallic body of the
        Jeff Koons ballerina
I looked into her eyes and saw the word *garden*

...

Each morning begins with a hypothesis: let this day be sown for the
        future we refer to as summer's last flowering
Not a tenderness but a thirst for certainty such that I know I have a
        body, a pair of hands pricked while deadheading the roses
A pair of hands exceeding the Tyrant, a pain that sustains itself long
        after the Philosopher had been reduced to ash

.

I had been appointed, the official letter had said, not the role of my
        district's wife or child but the role of one of the Tyrant's
        mistresses

.

Virtual reality effacing time's boundaries: entering my apartment to find
        its interiors over-written with the severe elegance of the Tyrant's
        favored Augustan Third Style: blue-black walls with slender
        columns and candelabra populated by tiny fantastic creatures
Vanished: my desk and my books
The Tyrant piercing the ballerina's metallic body and wandering her
        garden and piercing the trees and piercing the deer and piercing
        the shining river, the roses, the earth and its worm and piercing
        and piercing and piercing

...

Chapter TEN

Regardless of appearance there is birth and there is death

There is being and non-being

Interior and exterior

Disrobing with one hand, shielding with the other my sex, after the first
      night with the Tyrant I woke to my body furred as a leopard

Giving rise to new gestures and abilities of violence

Around my right thigh, a garland of bees

So many things needed saying in the garden but it was plummeting and
      scorching

Whether we are human or animal, animal or machine, machine or
      information: all at once permeated with doubt

   .

To run my hand once again over the Philosopher's sentences

To hold to cold marble my flushed cheek

...

On screen a woman walks through a museum in an advertisement for
      sepia washes, bleached-out fields of white evoking the spirit of
      Muybridge
The archive of Western art pillaged for virtual reality skins
The foundation of a photograph indistinguishable from its referent: the
      branded photograph of a hide marked with a cattle brand
Today I wear a body by Vermeer, round face, seashell ears with their
      attendant pearls garnered from Dutch colonial waters
And for my apartment: walls and windows gridded with Malevich's *Black
      Square*
Wearing the self-portrait of Parmigianino I did not feel like
      Parmigianino, and wearing Courbet I did not feel like Courbet,
      but with Schiele I felt his self-portrait's wracked body, organic
      twist
Stop playing games Phryne, the Tyrant said, returning the apartment
      back to the severe elegance of Augustan Third Style, and don't
      think for a moment, he said, I'll let you alone if you wear the
      body of a boy

    .

Now that summer is here there is little planting to be done
The walls when he leaves an undulating sea

...

In celebration of the coming solstice California sunsets are projected
      each evening across the city although the word *California* has
      been officially banned
On the bluff the Philosopher touches me again with his paper hands and
      his mouth tastes like sour milk and both dry and too much like
      sex and it is nearly impossible to reconcile this image with the
      last image, the image of the Philosopher an old man in bed
      slowly dying

      .

Each morning a hypothesis awakens but in June there is little planting to
      be done
Only family allowed to visit the elder home had said, but what family
Located in the former heartland, New City is to have ocean views
Regarding a statue in *contrapposto* we say her right hip, her right hand
      covering her womanhood, thus granting the sculpture
      subjectivity
Inserted into my dreamlife: a recurring snippet wherein the Philosopher
      stands from his wheelchair and smiling disembowels himself
      with a table knife as the camera pans to the Tyrant who stands
      and applauds

      .

How do I order this vocabulary raked and pruned, revealing a fern-like
      growth
One must not, the Tyrant says, touch the bodies of innocents
Revising our orientation we practice the imagined standpoint of the
      statue

...

In silver lamé I am Gerhard Richter's *Woman Descending a Staircase* and
        unable to undo the atrocities of our times
Categories denatured, as heat denatures fragile protein
Each identity we try on stays with us long after the virtual experience has
        worn off
As if, fern-like, we acquired a system of spores capable of manufacturing
        beyond the capacities of the usual industrial machinery
Are we surprised at the great measure of relief in this, for what is love
        but bright germination

     .

Virtual Reality technology has revised my route to the university such
        that I walk burning through burning buildings to the sea and
        then walk through the waves until still burning I arrive at my
        desk

...

As if what we believe depends on casting parts of one's own body in
       plaster and then recasting each sculpture in a more durable
       synthetic

Entering the gala on the Tyrant's arm I was all crinoline and corset
       under buttercup-yellow satin, beauty mark, silver Marie
       Antoinette wig

The theorized split between mind and body breaks down as we admit
       that even Descartes didn't know how to make his way through
       the pleats of matter, couldn't have guided us through the very
       last of the hydrangea ever to flower

The Philosopher joining a line of philosophers who correspond
       ardently with women in whom they say they see a bright
       reflection, a bright germination

    .

Translator and scribe but of whose narrative

    .

To have been corresponded with, to have entered the gala on a Tyrant's
       arm

...

There was of course a string quartet and waiters passing with finger-food
      and champagne
I was of course nodding to questions and I was smiling
I was balancing a small garden in my hair, complete with miniature
      android bees
I was growing warm in my crinoline and corset
And I was laughing in a polite way and then all of a sudden I was pulling
      a pistol from my satin handbag as if it were perfectly natural to
      be standing next to the Tyrant at a gala, and to be done up as
      Marie Antoinette pulling a pistol from her handbag with her
      calf-skin gloved hand
And the weight of the pistol in my hand all at once sent through me the
      idea of thought as a solution in which submerged substances
      disappear, and thought as a suspension in which particles settle
      into multi-colored layers, and thought as a dispersion in which
      particles maintain separate identities as they float away from
      their source
I then turned to the Tyrant and shot into his soft chest

...

If "to know" is to represent accurately what is outside the mind, then
        sentences become skin-like, what we believe depending on
        surface phenomena coloring the sky
The gaze of the taxidermy deer covered over in crystal spheres
        contributing to the stiffness of my speech, a stiffness of
        crinoline
And after: the Tyrant was on the ground, blood pooling
Or the Tyrant was on the ground, then jumping up saying to the crowd,
        to me: *darling, darling take a bow*

...

Chapter ELEVEN

I had acted of my own accord or had I acted according to the Tyrant

The Tyrant had died or the Tyrant had pulled off yet another illusion

Models of the temple show that when approached from the front the

    Aphrodite of Knidos modestly shields her womanhood from view

Move a few paces to the right and Phryne's gaze meets your gaze, her

    hand now coyly pointing to her sex

    .

The Earth we considered gracious for its heat-carrying ocean currents,

    its water-carrying air currents, and then we negated it

...

How to know who or what any given action will benefit or destroy
Praxiteles' Phryne famous not only for the absent statue he carved in her
      image but for her indecency trial forwarded through time for its
      exceptional oratory
To have been walking a sparsely populated island and come upon a
      garden of abandoned statues, female torsos disintegrating into
      sand, foreheads encircled by coronets, a pair of thighs, star-
      patterned pubic hair
To have been accused by a former lover of holding a shameless ritual
      procession, of organizing mixed-sex meetings, of introducing
      a new god who might have been Dionysus or Helios or Pluto
Some of the statues bearing the violence of cuts and blows, some
      deformed by natural weathering
To have stood in court before them in your blue robe understanding
      your influence as mistress, understanding the penalty would be
      death

    .

Meanwhile on the radio: the phrase *kill bird* and then static

...

The internal density of a liquid, when contained, retains a shape as
        distinct as a solid for every portion of matter is a garden
The butterfly, for example, had been folded into the caterpillar, its
        expulsion ending in a riot of orange and white and black
Another fluidity: the iris divides and replants, water beads across glass,
        the hide-and-seek between meaning and form carrying on
A rumor that hackers had modified the skin's code such that it is
        possible the virtual reality gun had shot real bullets
Upon suspecting an unfavorable verdict the orator, who like Phryne's
        accuser had at one time been her lover, famously defends her
        by tearing from her her robes, inspiring within the judges the
        fear of Aphrodite
The next state of being will accentuate fluidity, call our attention to the
        many moments we are poised between life and death

   .

A video clip circulates of the Tyrant parading around the ballroom and
        then buckling in real pain, real blood

   .

A consolation leaving agency unresolved

   .

Her gold belt pooling on the ground, blue robe flying above her a wing

...

The Tyrant after his attempted assassination testifying to a rebirth,
a revelation
Or someone donning the body of the Tyrant after his assassination
testifying to a rebirth, a revelation broadcast across all the
citizens' screens
To consider every branch of every plant to be likewise a garden: chives,
mint, and other soft-leaved subjects kept viable in deep freeze
The Tyrant calling on human mothers to be implanted with non-human
embryos
Should a plant yellow it will be lifted and burnt, in this way we might
develop a muscular concept of matter
This birth project he calls an act of global patriotism visioned at the
moment of death
Faith that language has an immediate connection with materiality
articulated by Pliny the Elder's conviction that plumbago, from
"plumbum," meaning "lead," could cure lead poisoning
Again extinct species might live, again we might have deer, bees,
although the Philosopher and California are among the eternally
lost
The Tyrant still alive or the virtual reality skin of the Tyrant still alive

.

Once we had been certain that time functioned universally like a
mathematical truth in an order beyond our small transitory
gardens
Lead-blue flowers and sap leaving the cure of lead-colored marks on
skin

...

To love as if there was no such thing as love, only two people in an
      emptied room

In the *Naturalis* Pliny the Elder suggests Phryne's statue was so beautiful
      men would break into the temple to make love to it at night,
      leaving a stain along her thigh

Like wetness, time clings to individual bodies, comes into agreement
      only when these bodies are not moving and thus there is no
      certainty

How else to explain accounts of blemished marble when we know the
      statue to have been made of purity

Plumbago, tender, non-invasive, can safely be planted next to
      foundations

.

In another version it was a single nobleman so taken with Phryne's
      statue that he dedicated all his possessions to the goddess,
      carved her name on every tree, stole into her temple night after
      night, masturbating to her image

Regardless of its name plumbago, tender, singes in full sun

.

According to townspeople the nobleman one day launched himself over
      the cliff and drowned in the sea

...

In another version of the trial Phryne, suspecting an unfavorable verdict,
     herself bares her breasts
Or Phryne, born poor but having as *hetaera,* courtesan, mistress
     amassed considerable wealth purchases a favorable verdict
Or Phryne, clutching modestly closed her blue robe kneels and begs for
     her life
What will the future say of these fallen goddesses
When I returned home my walls were walls, my books returned, my desk
     a desk, my reflection unaugmented, human

...

To gain again the deer and the bee and if this time birthed from humans
      would we love them more, hold them as bright germination
Windows looking out at rubble, broken satellite dishes, the sea metallic,
      turgid
Cast out of the garden or released from the garden

    .

Step close to any figure, small or large, and its material will fragment
      flickering and light

"& dreamed again:" "The tyrant floated" "in a blue sky"

—Alice Notley, *Descent of Alette*

Sources:

Domus: Wall Painting in the Roman House. Donatella Mazzoleni and
      Umberto Pappalardo, 2005
EXTOXNET, Extension Toxicology Database
Gardening Week by Week. Xenia Field, 1975
Matter. Ralph E. Lapp and the Editors of Time-Life Books, 1969
Natural History: A Selection. Gaius Plinius Secundus, translated by John F.
      Healy, 1991
On Certainty. Ludwig Wittgenstein, translated by Denis Paul and G.E.M.
      Anscombe, 1969
Phryne before the Areopagus. Jean-Léon Gérôme, 1861
*Roman Frescoes from Boscoreale: The Villa of Publius Fannius Synistor in Reality
      and Virtual Reality.* Bettina Bergmann, Stefano De Caro, Joan R.
      Mertens, and Rudolf Meyer, 2010
The Art of the Body: Antiquity and Its Legacy. Michael Squire, 2011
The Fold: Leibniz and the Baroque. Gilles Deleuze, translated by Tom
      Conley, 1992
The Letters of the Younger Pliny. Pliny the Younger, translated by Betty
      Radice, 1963
The Mesothelioma Center at Asbestos.com
The Union Carbide Corporation Website
"Wildest Dreams: Douglas Coupland Talks with Daniel Birnbaum about
      Art and Virtual Reality," *Artforum,* 2017

Acknowledgements:

Thank you to the following editors for publishing selections from this manuscript, often in a variant form: Kristina Marie Darling for *Tupelo Quarterly*, Paul Hoover for *New American Writing;* Brenda Iijima for *GUEST [a journal of guest editors]*; and Bradford Morrow for *Conjunctions.* Rusty Morrison, Laura Joakimson, and all of Omnidawn: thank you for this book and for the light you pour into the world. For Ken Keegan: eternal gratitude. Thank you to G.C. Waldrep for reading and commenting on an early draft. Thank you, Alan Gilbert, for your companionship, brilliance, and generosity.

Karla Kelsey's books include *Blood Feather* (Tupelo Press, 2020); *Of Sphere,* selected by Carla Harryman for the Essay Press Prize (2017); *A Conjoined Book* (Omnidawn, 2014); *Iteration Nets* (Ahsahta, 2010); and *Knowledge Forms, the Aviary,* selected by Carolyn Forché for the Sawtooth Poetry Prize (Ahsahta, 2006). A recipient of awards and fellowships from the Poetry Society of America, the Fulbright Scholars Program, and Yale University, she serves on the faculty of Susquehanna University and with Aaron McCollough co-publishes SplitLevel Texts.

On Certainty

by Karla Kelsey

Cover art: Cubiculum (bedroom) from the Villa of P. Fannius Synistor at Boscoreale. The Metropolitan Museum of Art, New York. Rogers Fund, 1903. www.metmuseum.org/art/collection/search/247017

Cover design by Laura Joakimson
Interior design by Laura Joakimson
Cover typeface: Athelas
Interior typeface: Athelas and Garamond

Printed in the United States
by Books International, Dulles, Virginia

Publication of this book was made possible in part by gifts from Katherine & John Gravendyk in honor of Hillary Gravendyk, Francesca Bell, Mary Mackey, and The New Place Fund

Omnidawn Publishing Oakland, California

Staff and Volunteers, Fall 2023

Rusty Morrison senior editor & co-publisher
Laura Joakimson, executive director and co-publisher
Rob Hendricks, poetry & fiction editor, & post-pub marketing
Jason Bayani, poetry editor
Anthony Cody, poetry editor
Liza Flum, poetry editor
Kimberly Reyes, poetry editor
Sharon Zetter, poetry editor & bookdesigner
Jeffrey Kingman, copy editor
Jennifer Metsker, marketing assistant
Sophia Carr, marketing assistant
Katie Tomzynski, marketing assistant